POLISHING THE MIRROR:
90 Days to Vocational Clarity

by Jennifer L. Manlowe, PhD

For my sister
Laury Payne Bryant
(18 July 1961)

PROLOGUE

For many centuries, mystics across the globe have been fascinated with the poetic metaphor of *polishing the mirror*. What did this mean? Why did they urge others to reflect upon this active metaphor? Here are a few examples:

"Dear friend, your heart is a polished mirror. You must wipe it clean of the veil of dust that has gathered upon it because it is destined to reflect the light of divine secrets. "
~ *al-Ghazzali*

"There is a polish for everything, and the polish for the heart Is the remembrance of God." ~ *Muhammad*

"Everyone sees the Unseen in proportion to the clarity of her heart, and that depends upon how much she has polished it. Whoever has polished it more sees more—more unseen forms become manifest to her." ~ *Rumi*

"An unexamined life is not worth living." ~ *Socrates*

"Let go of your worries and be completely clear-hearted, like the face of a mirror that contains no images. When empty of forms, all forms are contained within it. No face would be ashamed to be so clear." ~ *Rumi*

Myths too have been used as ethical warnings about being preoccupied with our own reflection: Narcissus[1] from the Greek myth was considered to be a beautiful youth who rejected the nymph Echo and fell in love with his own reflection mirrored in a pool. He pined away and was punished by being changed into the flower that bears his name. The mermaid—a mythical half-human sea creature with the head and trunk of a woman and the tail of a fish, conventionally depicted as beautiful woman with long, flowing, golden hair with a mirror in one hand and comb in the other. She, too, was considered "trapped in a trance" and a seductive-siren role that consistently lead sailors to their death.

You might be asking yourself, "How might I use this *mirror metaphor* in a non-narcissistic way. Is there a way to learn

_____

[1] In Greek, *narke* means "numb"

more about myself in relation to others in this 90-day journal that is all about my vocational clarity?" What if I don't relate to these myths or mystics?

Whether you relate to them or not doesn't matter. Let their invitation to become clear-hearted be a path to your vocation.

As a creative career counselor, author and world-traditions educator, I find that one need not be a believer of any one religious tradition to reap the benefits of their poetic power. As a matter of fact, "getting clear" about what we are here to do—our vocation—has often been the domain of philosophers not priests. Socrates, via his student Plato, and Aristotle wrote volumes on "values," "life-direction," "soulful truthfulness" and "authentic purpose."

Many ancient world philosophers invited their students to consider these five questions that you will be considering in this brief journal:

Who am I?

What am I here to do?

What matters most in this world?

What are my obligations to others?

What is Love?

Though this book is based on modern experiences of those who have felt "in-between" worlds after losing a job or experiencing a significant shift in their life's direction, this kind of vocational search is not a new concern. As a matter of fact, the term "vocation"—meaning a strong feeling of suitability for a particular purpose in life—has ancient roots. It comes from the Latin word *vocare* ("to call")—and discerning this call feels like a great mystery to most of us. Socrates called this part of himself his divine sign or guide. Like his mother who was a midwife, he saw himself birthing wisdom that he believed was already present in his students.

Believing that we can "hear our calling" may feel as farfetched as believing that we can simply put our ear up to a conch shell for navigation. And yet author Sivananda Radha writes that such a practice can be fruitful:

"Listening to the conch shell is like listening to the still, small voice within. The mind must be still to be able to hear this soft voice."

This insightful journal is an invitation to cultivate clarity for "what's next" in your life. It will help you listen to that voice within you, the voice that will nudge you along toward your right work in the world, your vocation. "Polishing the mirror" becomes code for cultivating calm, stilling your thoughts, dusting off social conditioning, and letting go of anxiousness about the future. These helpful writing techniques and clever questions help you uncover your hidden passions, psycho-social temperament and natural talents, which, in turn, give you an increasingly sharp focus for going forward. Give it 90-days-in-a-row and judge for yourself!

Personally, I would pick up this journal and use it in a daily way, as regularly as polishing anything that needs dusting. Why? This writing can be a meditation in and of itself.

One student named Meredith writes: "When I'm cleaning, many thoughts drift up within me and I realize that important cleaning and clearing out gets done in me, too.

My thoughts move about flowing in a stream of consciousness, resting momentarily on anything that needs a little dusting and polishing. I examine these thoughts, and then try to let them go."

When we reflect upon how we see ourselves, and all things, there is so much wisdom to find. I'm figuring that you can give it a try for 90 days, right? That's about 10 minutes a day. Scientists say that any habit can be ingrained after practicing it for 90 days straight. Why not test out this theory?

They say a change of habit will help you align your actions and desires. Too often we want something, but our actions don't match up.

Scientists say it takes this long to change a habit because we often resist change. According to yoga teachings, it takes 40 days to change a bad habit into a positive one but 90 days to have the new habit become yours.

As you'll see, this journal will invite you to cultivate clarity in ways that work beyond your best thinking. These questions will work **for** you and **on** you in a daily, experiential, and intuitive way. You'll be inspired to reflect and write briefly, just one-paragraph-a-day, as a way to begin or end each day. Through cultivating this 90-day habit, my hope is that you will witness simple—even profound—changes unfolding in your life that produce authentic vocational clarity.

Taking just "one day at a time" has been a technique that has helped millions of people all over the globe experience positive shifts in their lives. Apparently, some of us are just like ants; what may look like big changes to the outsider is, for the insider, virtually unnoticeable. Yet progress is made and seems to be the result of millions of small, deliberate actions taken on a moment-by-moment basis.

We may not see such changes happening in our lives because we are too close to our daily choices, and our shifts in attitude and behavior. But, we are like ants, simply part of an invisible web, a truly revolutionary process called "cultivating clarity." So, keep notes in this journal; it will help you track your progress and, later, bear witness to almost all your shifts in thinking, doing and feeling. You may not notice the scales dropping from your eyes but you will begin to feel these changes in your being.

By reflecting upon these daily quotes, poems, and philosophical axioms, and by being called into action through these simple questions, you may feel ready to write about how these ideas work on you, work for you, and provoke you to **see, hear** and **live** a little bit differently.

Let your mind and heart reflect for a few moments on what comes to you after reading each quotation and then move on to unselfconsciously fill in the blank page beneath each inspirational invitation. As I say to my students and clients: "Your progress, like your investment in this course, is all up to you."

I find that "seeking vocational clarity" does not mean trying hard to find it. By being curious and open, clarity, in time, will find us. Or more accurately, the wisdom that was inside all along begins to shine through and we're more able to reflect such wisdom in those around us.

AN INVITATION

To make the most of your time and energy, start this journal at anytime but keep moving through it day after day until day 90. If you miss a day, start over. Refine the answers to the initial questions. Stick with it. Keep starting over if you can't stay with your commitment, this new habit, yourself. You see, you are building self-trust, integrity and intimacy with yourself and thereby becoming more trustworthy, reliable and capable of intimacy with others. No matter what, these questions will be working on you and in you. They will evoke or provoke your inner wisdom, your intuition and crystal-clear nature. If you want it to, this journal might help you:

- Get clarity regarding you talents & passions
- Transform your fears and doubts into positive tools

- Set target dates for what you want your life to look like
- Build a vision-board (a two-dimensional "collage" of your hopes and dreams for a fuller/simpler life).
- Deepen your capacity to feel a quiet calm and ease even while being attentive to who and what matters most
- Shake loose social baggage that no longer speaks to you
- Invite you to remember to celebrate progress all along the way

ACKNOWLEDGMENTS

Thanks to all of my friends and family who offered quotes and support for this journal. Laury Bryant, Susan Kuebler, C.J. Dorgeloh, Melinda Manlowe, Lesley Collins, Whitney Bennett, Jan Schwer, LeeAnn Gibbs, Janine Fixmer, Rob Overton, Yvonne Bleiman, Carrie West, Danielle Doughman, Tracy Lawrence, Valerie Young, and my beloved, Tony Fairbank.

READY, SET, GO!

What are you waiting for? Are there any obstacles arising in you as you think about going forward with cultivating a more rewarding life in a simple, straightforward and one-page-a-day way? List them here:

Day 1

"What do you want your life to look and feel like?"
~ Valerie Young

What 10 changes do you want to see happen in your life this year? Make sure you place the date on it so you can see what happens every 30 days—it might work like magic. No need to be "a believer," just be willing, like any scientist, to experiment.

1.   2.

3.   4.

5.   6.

7.   8.

9.   10.

Day 2

"The very act of considering your explorations worth keeping track of begins to change everything you ever thought about yourself." ~ *Barbara Sher*

What are three things you want to know more about? List them here. Find an 8½ by 11-inch envelope to store images, essays or articles that pique your interests about these questions of yours.

Day 3

"Baby Suggs—the preacher in the woods—told the newly-freed slaves that the only grace they could have was the grace they could imagine. That if they could not see it, they would not have it." ~ *Toni Morrison*

What is the life you envision for yourself? Write (in the 1½ pages here) how you would start and end your day in this life. Be thick with your description because "If you cannot see it, you will not have it!"

Keep going: What is the life you envision for yourself?

Day 4

"There are two great days in a person's life—the day we are born and the day we discover why." ~ *William Barclay*

For most of us, feeling like we don't know why we are here is a fragmenting feeling—we can feel like a broken kaleidoscope. What are the fragments in you or in your life right now that you seem to be juggling?

Day 5

"You cannot create a statue by smashing the marble with a hammer, and you cannot by force of arms release the essence of a person." ~ *Confucius*

What in your life do you feel you are forcing right now? Why not give up control right now? Next month, look back to this page to see how the letting go of control has helped you.

Day 6

"The lilies of the field and the birds of the air struggle not, for they know that their heavenly provider has allotted them everything they need each day." ~ *Matthew 6:27-30*

Look at your life right now and everything you have ever done to be where you are at this point in time. What needs do you have? What is absolutely divine or perfect just as it is right now?

Day 7

"Your greatest pleasure is that which rebounds from the hearts that you have made glad." ~ *Henry Ward Beecher*

If you were going to surprise someone with a gift today, what would that gift be? What gift would you want to receive? Who might you ask to give to you the gift(s) you want to receive?

Day 8

"Thoughts become things. So be careful what you think."
~ Denis Waitley

How you talk to yourself can send out powerful messages.
Write down some thoughts you wish you would stop
thinking. Which new thoughts would you like to practice
including in an effort to build a stronger foundation for
your inner sanctum?

Day 9

"It is almost as important to know what is not serious as to know what is." ~ *John Kenneth Galbraith*

If you are hearing a clock ticking on your goals in life, what keeps you from actualizing them? What reason do you give yourself or others for your action or inaction? How is that working for you AND against you?

Day 10

"Let's stop the [gospel] singing and start the swinging...
this revolution is going to happen by any means
necessary." ~ Malcolm X

What needs radical change in the world today? What needs
change in your life right now?

Day 11

"We can't solve problems by using the same kind of thinking we used when we created them." ~ *Albert Einstein*

Is there anything that you are struggling with that you feel your best thinking cannot solve? How would someone you admire solve this problem?

Day 12

"Each time you judge yourself you break your heart."
~ *Kirpal Vananji*

Judging ourselves is our greatest enemy. Write down below your worst mistake (in code if you must) on this very page. Does it still seem to be a big deal? If so, can amend your mistake?

Day 13

"Remembering that the way to get somewhere is to take one step at a time changes immobility to progress."
~ Barbara Sher

Can you give yourself ten minutes of variety today? What would that look like? Describe or draw it here.

Day 14

"The best way to make your dreams come true is to wake up."
~ *Paul Valery*

After the events of September 11th 2001, many people from the U.S. felt a wake-up call to live a more informed and meaning-filled life. What might you plant today (even in your imagination) that you would like to see take root, no matter what tomorrow may hold? Describe its features.

Day 15

"Life is no brief candle to me. It is a sort of splendid torch which I have got hold of for the moment, and I want to make it burn as brightly as possible before handing it on to future generations." ~ *George Bernard Shaw*

How do you bring a candle to the room of your own mind?

Day 16

"Patients are not cured by free association, they are cured when they can freely associate." ~ *Sandor Ferenczi*

Ferenczi's approach was unique at this time (the early 1900s) because he believed that digging or uncovering the past to resolve conflicts was tantamount to digging downward to get out of a hole. What in your present life do you think might benefit from a 180-degree shift in worldview?

Day 17

"It's not what's happening to you or in you; it's how you relate to what is happening that matters."
~ Joseph Goldstein

How are you relating to your life and your loved ones' right now? What's truly miraculous about these connections? Describe this miracle as if you were describing it to a third-grader.

Day 18

"The key to integrating a meditation practice into our daily lives is to take up regular practice every day, for a little while and you need to connect with others to do this, it's challenging." ~ *Trudy Goodman*

Creating a life where you feel a greater sense of calm and clarity isn't always easy. Why not try four days of 10-minutes of sitting and listening to the sound of your exhales—like ocean waves in a conch shell—while staring out a window. How is that practice for you?

Day 19

"Before you tell your life what you intend to do with it, listen for what it intends to do with you." ~ *Parker Palmer*

As you sit quietly for 10-minutes, ask your life what it intends to do with you? Just take a wild guess and write about it here.

Day 20

"All truly wise thoughts have been thought already thousands of times; but to make them truly ours, we must think them over again honestly, till they take root in our personal experience." - *Johann Wolfgang von Goethe*

When you look back over the past three weeks, what has helped you stick with this writing and reflecting challenge? Being willing to start over, from the beginning, can be a really interesting way to help uncover your wisest thoughts.

Day 21

"What is asking for attention and acceptance just now."
~ Eugene Gendlin

Take 10 minutes to just listen to your bodily sensations (without the storyline) before writing. What needs attending to and accepting as it is right now?

Day 22

"Peace is not something you can force... It is like trying to quiet the ocean by pressing upon the waves. Sanity lies in somehow opening to the chaos, allowing anxiety, moving deeply into the tumult, diving into the waves, where underneath, within, peace simply is." ~ *Gerald May*

Set your egg timer (or your watch) for 10 minutes. See what it is like to just stare and let your mind drift away. Afterward, write what it was like to have no particular focus.

Day 23

"Better keep yourself clean and bright; you are the window through which you must see the world."
~ George Bernard Shaw

What do you notice needs *wise attention* in the world around you; in your larger human family; in your particular locale? What would it be like to just do one thing that made a small difference? What would dust off some of the dullness you see within and around you?[2]

---

[2] Do you want some ideas? Checkout: www.climatecrisis.net

Day 24

"Most of the shadows of this life are caused by standing in one's own sunshine." ~ *Ralph Waldo Emerson*

If you had a theatrical call-back to take part in a performance that you knew as well as your own phone number, but there was only one stipulation, you had to describe what others might call your brightest lights or what Emerson speaks of as "your own sunshine," what would you convey?

Day 25

"Getting stuck in the wrong career is like a horror movie where I've been buried and no one can hear my screams!"
~ *Barbara Sher*

Describe, in detail, the absolutely wrong career for you. How does the day start, who is involved, how is time spent there and how does it end?

Day 26

"Choose an occupation you love and you'll never have to work a day in your life." ~ *Confucius*

Write down some examples of what you've been told you should do with your life according to your family members, teachers, religious leaders or peers.

Day 27

"Whenever you're thinking about making any big career decisions, change the word *commit* to the words *try out* or *audition* a career." ~ *Barbara Sher*

List 10 things that you do when you simply lose track of time (it's even okay to have one of them be watching TV). Next to your 10 things you simply love to do, write 10 jobs where people get paid to do these things.

Day 28

"Through all the world there goes one long cry from the heart of the artist: *Only give me the chance to do my very best!*" ~ Isak Dinesen

What in your life are you giving your very best? How does that make you feel? How does your energy affect those around you? Where might you bring fuller engagement to your actions today?

Day 29

"We can't move forward if we forget to celebrate from whence we've come." ~ *Jennifer Manlowe*

Make a list of the progress you've made this month. What experiences and accomplishments, big and small, have you made this month? It's time to take a bow and share some of these accomplishments with a "back-patter" type of person or friend.

Day 30

"What we learn to do we learn by doing." ~ *Aristotle*

Describe one of the biggest lessons that you are learning-by-doing in this 90-day experiment. If this day was just one slice of pie, what kind of pie would it be and why?

Day 31

"Keep knocking and the joy inside will eventually open a window and look out to see who's there." ~ *Rumi*

If you were a joy-filled person, what would be important to you? How would you know that joy has arrived?

Day 32

"Regret for the things we did can be tempered by time; it is regret for the things we did not do that is inconsolable."
~ *Sydney J. Harris*

No matter what your age, it's never too late to do that thing you wish you did before. What would you do if you were a billionaire and you could afford to do anything with your life?

Day 33

"Fall seven times, stand up eight." ~ *Daruma Daishi*

As you look back on your life, is there a time in the past when you fell and refused to get back up? What about that choice was comfortable?

Day 34

"We read the world wrong and say that it deceives us."
~ Rabindranath Tagore

As you look at the daily news do you feel deceived? As you look around you, do you feel you are seeing accurately? What helps you discern the true from the false?

Day 35

"You do not have to be good. You do not have to walk on your knees for a hundred miles through the desert, repenting. You only have to let the soft animal of your body love what it loves." ~ *Mary Oliver*

As a person who was raised in a very religious home, I didn't know there was another way to approach the world outside of martyring myself to be good. Today, I practice **not** apologizing for loving what I love. What do you *really* love?

Day 36

"The difference between a good life and a bad life is how well you walk through the fire." ~ C.G. Jung

Is anything burning for you right now? What is the fire you are walking through this year, so far?

Day 37

"To go in the dark with a light is to know the light. To know the dark, go dark. Go without sight, and find that the dark, too, blooms and sings, and is traveled by dark feet and dark wings." ~ *Wendell Berry*

Can you bring the light to the feelings of *going dark?* Give an example of that here.

Day 38

"A people's ability to grow and succeed is largely related to their ability to suffer embarrassment."
~ Doug Engelbart

When was the last time you were embarrassed? What did you do or not do that made you feel exposed? What was that like for you?

Day 39

"In those years, people will say we lost track of the meaning of We.... We found ourselves reduced to I and the whole thing became silly, ironic, terrible." ~ *Adrienne Rich*

If you have relatives who have died, how might they read the social, psychological and spiritual trends in this particular moment? What would they want you to know?

Day 40

"Trying is dying." ~ *Anonymous*

Is there a place in your life that doesn't seemed to be helped by your trying and trying to change it? What would a 180° reversal of your present technique look and feel like?

Day 41

"Can human beings lose the density of their conditioned mind structures and become like crystals or precious stones... transparent to the light of consciousness?"
~ Eckhart Tolle

What makes you feel more alive and open, less dense, less bogged down by heavy thoughts and feelings?

Day 42

"Every breath is a sacrament, an affirmation of our connection with all other living things, a renewal of our link with our ancestors and a contribution to generations yet to come." ~ *David Suzuki*

Which situations in your life might benefit if you were to remember to breathe? What might jog your memory in this regard?

Day 43

"The first serious impediment to the growth of authentic love between the sexes is the sentimental, romantic way we think about love." ~ *Sam Keen*

Do you think about love? How do you think about it? How do you know that you feel it or have it or give it or receive it? What helps or hinders your sense of love?

Day 44

"Act only according to that maxim whereby you can at the same time *will* that it should become a universal law."
~ *Immanuel Kant*

As you look around you at what you call "the world you live in," what ways do you act that could be come a *universal law*—those ways of being that would be good for all the creatures who live on the planet?

Day 45

"I do the thing which nature drives me to do. Does a fish know in which water that he swims?" ~ *Einstein*

What are some things that "nature" seems to be driving you to do?

Day 46

"Action stops fear." ~ *Margaret Bourke-White*

Describe a situation in your life today that calls you to take action instead of recoil in fear.

Day 47

"Think of life as a terminal illness, because if you do, you will live it with joy and passion as it ought to be lived."
~ Anna Quindlen

Take some time to reflect on how you see your own passion, your own creativity and your own fire. Does an image come to mind? Are there colors? Don't censor your writing; just notice what emerges.

Day 48

"If we were meant to make this [life on this ship] a true home, we would have a monumental adjustment to make, and only our companions on this ship to look to. We must turn to each other, and sense that this is possible."
~ Barry Lopez

Who are your closest companions? Who do you turn to in your effort to create this *true home*?

Day 49

"It seems only yesterday I used to believe there was nothing under my skin but light. If you cut me I could shine. But now when I fall upon the sidewalks of life, I skin my knees. I bleed." ~ *Billy Collins*

Was there a time in your life when you might have called yourself, "innocent," or "magical," or "naïve"? Write about that time? What was going on then? If your attitude about this has changed, what changes have occurred to shift your thinking?

Day 50

"I think it important to try to see the present calamity in a true perspective. We are mistaken when we compare war with *normal life*. Life has never been normal."
~ C.S. Lewis

As you look within and around you, what about any conflicts you witness, or that you are part of, seem normal? Why is that so? Might there be something you would do to bring greater peace—in a way, adding a sense of abnormality to a situation that has become mundane?

Day 51

"Whenever loss occurs, we can either resist or yield. Yielding means inner acceptance of what is. You are open to life. Resistance is an inner contraction; you are closed. When you surrender, a new dimension of consciousness opens up." ~ *Eckhart Tolle*

Does surrendering to a feeling that you have heretofore resisted seem to affect your level of happiness? Why or why not?

Day 52

"Tell me, what is it you plan to do with your one wild and precious life?" ~ *Mary Oliver*

What is precious about your life right now? What might you do with your life to live more closely to your natural sense of wildness?

Day 53

"The blizzard of the world has crossed the threshold, and overturned the order of the soul." ~ *Leonard Cohen*

Do you feel crushed by the world's blizzards? How so? Why not? What seems to help you bounce back, dig yourself out and get back into working with the snowstorms of life?

Day 54

"We can make our minds so like still water that beings gather about us that they may see, it may be, their own images, and so live for a moment with a clearer, perhaps even with a fiercer life because of our quiet."
~ *William Butler Yeats*

What is helping you cultivate a sense of inner quiet? As you look about you, who is drawn to you when you feel still inside?

Day 55

"The soul empties itself of all its own contents in order to receive into itself the being it is looking at—just as he or she is, in all his or her truth." ~ *Simone Weil*

When you feel emptied of all that you used to be attached to, how do you feel? How might you practice receiving today?

Day 56

"I am being driven forward
Into an unknown land....
Shall I ever get there?
There where life resounds
A clear pure note
In the silence?" ~ *Dag Hammarskjold*

Where is "there" for you? How will you know? What do you
expect to feel when you get there?

Day 57

"In a genuine relationship, there is an outward flow of open, alert attention toward the other person in which there is no wanting whatsoever. That alert attention is Presence. It is the prerequisite for any authentic relationship." ~ *Eckhart Tolle*

What helps you cultivate attention toward another? Do you wait your turn to speak? Are you interested in getting something from the other? Try listening with Presence?

Day 58

"A daily dose of pleasure can help you bounce back from life's pressures" ~ *Al Siebert*

Here, (**and on a separate piece of paper**), list 10 actions that easily give you joy. Place this list right by your telephone and read it (and add to it) every time you receive or make a phone call.

1.
2.
3.
4.
5.
6.
7.
8.
9.
10.

Day 59

"This map of my dream life is amazing. I colored it, added photos from magazines, even stitched some yarn into the corner to remind me of my favorite form of creating with my hands." ~ *Linda R.*

Spend no more than a few dollars on a 24" X 36" piece of poster board. Lay this poster out flat and begin placing upon it images, article titles, favorite quotes, whatever speaks to your soulful self in your effort to SEE what you love about the current life you have and the life you would have if you had more of what you love in it. This is called a "vision board" and it works like magic to make you conscious of your thoughts and wishes. I've seen most of these dreams come true for myself, and my clients, year after year. The unconscious works in mysterious ways.[3]

---

[3] See also Barbara Sher's www.wishcraft.com

Day 60

"It is a mistake to look too far ahead. Only one link in the chain of destiny can be handled at a time."
~ *Winston Churchill*

Take a look back to **Day One**'s list of ten wishes; if you haven't made them, now's your chance! Picking ten small changes—per wish—from this list, which change among them is the smallest action you might take to move your dreams forward?

Day 61

"Everyone's work shall be made manifest: for the day shall
declare it, because it shall be revealed by fire; and the fire
shall try everyone's work for what sort it is."
~ I Corinthians 3:13

Take some colored pens, pencils, or crayons and create a
picture of "fire." Let yourself play. What's revealed when
you look at what you've created? (Be sure to save this
image with this journal).

Day 62

"Happiness is thought to depend on leisure; for we are busy that we may have leisure." ~ *Aristotle*

How did your grandparents and parents think of "leisure"—time free of obligations? Did idleness indicate a lack of virtue? Some people experience "downtime" as literally *down* time; they need to be working, perhaps proving themselves worthy, to feel alive. Do you allow yourself time off? How do you feel when you do so?

Day 63

"The secret of human happiness is not in self-seeking but in self-forgetting." ~ *Theodor Reik*

Give what you want to receive...at least in prayer. Do you believe that life is like a boomerang, i.e., that whatever you do will come back to you? Give an example of this truism from your own history.

Day 64

"True friendship is a plant of slow growth, and must undergo and withstand the shocks of adversity before it is entitled to the appellation." ~ *George Washington*

How do you know when you've earned the title, *true friend*? When you think about someone you call a true friend, what traits come to mind?

Day 65

"The hand moves and the fire's
whirling takes different shapes.
All things change when we do." ~ *Kukai*

What helps you make a change in your thinking, attitude,
or behavior? Recollect a time when you had a particular
attachment or aversion to change? What happened?

Day 66

"Individuality is only possible if it unfolds from wholeness."
~ David Bohm

Is there someone you know who seems to be stuck in a rut?
If you were feeling half-alive, what would have to happen
for, in, or **to** you to awaken the other half of you?

Day 67

"If at first you don't succeed you're like everyone else who went on to greatness." ~ *Ray Bradbury*

Whom do you admire most and what part did failure fit into their life experience? If you were to "shadow" that person for 10 important years of their life, what would you learn?

Day 68

"There are a thousand ways to kneel and kiss the ground, there are a thousand ways to go home again." ~ *Rumi*

What are ways you "go home" to what is natural in your life? Do you let nature guide and support you? Write about what delights you in the natural world.

Day 69

"Our only enemies are guilt, fear and shame. Such unresolved negatives prevent us from living fully."
~ Elisabeth Kübler-Ross

What habits of thinking seem to be enemies for you? How do you know when they have been "acting up"? What slays the *gremlins* or at least arrests them so you might get on with the business of creating a fuller life?

Day 70

"I am the breeze that nurtures all things green… I am the rain coming from the dew that causes the grasses to laugh with the joy of life." ~ *Hildegard of Bingen*

Do you feel that you are part of the natural world?[4] Why or why not? What helps you experience this essential interdependence?

---

[4] Checkout "Outward Bound Wilderness" for hikers of all ages: www.outwardboundwilderness.org

Day 71

"If the doors of perception were cleansed, everything would appear to us as it is, infinite. For we have closed ourselves up, 'til we see all through the narrow chinks of our cavern." ~ *William Blake*

What wipes clean your doors of perception? How do you know when your view has become clouded? What actions can you take to cultivate clarity today?

Day 72

"The illusion of freedom is that it is getting away from things you don't like." ~ *Jerilyn Munyon*

From what do wish you could get free? Can you simply accept that thing, or habit, just as it is? Why or why not?

Day 73

"Failure is not an option. When you are truly aligned with your passions, nothing can stop you."
~ Janet & Chris Attwood

If you were to yield to the passions of your life, what would they be? Can you trust that your passions—like a golden thread—will lead you to your own truth, your own success? Write a Thank You note to each specific passion for guiding you every step of the way?

Day 74

"Separate reeds are weak and easily broken, but bound together they are strong and hard to tear apart."
~ *The Midrash*

Who in your surroundings knows and supports you? If you don't have a spiritually-nourishing community, how might you find or start one? Checkout www.meetup.com

Day 75

"Being an artist means not reckoning and counting, but ripening like the tree which does not force its sap and stands confident in the storms of spring without the fear that after them may come no summer." ~ *Rainer Maria Rilke*

If your fear and confidence were each a color, or a season, which would each be and why?

Day 76

"The world cannot be discovered by a journey of miles…
only by a spiritual journey by which we arrive at the ground
at our feet, and learn to be at home." ~ *Wendell Berry*

Which practices help you feel at home in your body? Which
habits help you feel connected to your loved ones, to your
neighbors, to your world?

Day 77

"Your proper concern is alone the *action* of duty, not the *fruits* of the action. Cast then away all desire and fear for the fruits and perform your duty." ~ *The Bhagavad-Gita*

How do you feel when you're in the flow of your right work? What helps you stay focused on what delights and enlivens you?

Day 78

"Life is being as it is." ~ *Joko Beck*

What is the difference between being and doing in your life and in your parents' life? Why is or isn't that an important distinction for you?

Day 79

"Everything that irritates us about others can lead us to an understanding of ourselves." ~ C.G. Jung

If there is someone from your past who seems to be "looking over your shoulder," who is that person? How does he or she find fault with you? If you're stuck, work backwards from this equation: Who, *out there*, really bugs or disgusts you? What traits do they share with you?

Day 80

"Some cause happiness wherever they go, others, whenever they go." ~ *Oscar Wilde*

Who in your life—or what traits of your own—do you wish would leave?

Day 81

"Many of life's failures are people who did not realize how close they were to success when they gave up."
~ Thomas Edison

How do you define success? How do you know when you're close to it? How do you get support to "never give up?"

Day 82

"A conversation is a dialogue, not a monologue. That's why there are so few good conversations."
~ *Truman Capote*

Just as an outrageous test, try to ask only "open and honest questions" today or don't speak at all...just listen and express yourself with your eyes and body gestures. Then, at the end of this day, write down your observations here.

Day 83

"Every time you suppress some part of yourself or allow others to play you small, you are in essence ignoring the owner's manual your creator gave you and destroying your design." ~ *Oprah Winfrey*

If you had an owner's manual, what section would you need to read or re-read in order to get a better understanding about how you run most smoothly? What might you learn?

Day 84

"Those who trim themselves to suit everyone will soon whittle away." ~ *Raymond Hull*

How do you know when you're playing small in a group or around a special person? What does it feel like in your body? Do you sweat more, shrink in your chair, talk in a baby voice or resist eye-contact? Tell a story about the last time you did that and why it was the **last** time.

Day 85

"Think about it. Can you think of one situation that is improved by being more tense?" ~ *Martha Beck*

Where in your life might you breathe more, relax more, consider resting more? Are these things easy or difficult for you to do?

Day 86

"Stand still.
The forest knows where you are.
You must let it find you." ~ *David Wagoner*

Where is there a nearby forest? Can you dress appropriately and go there this upcoming weekend? What happens when you stand still?

Day 87

"There are only two ways to live your life. One is as though nothing is a miracle, the other is as though everything is a miracle." ~ *Albert Einstein*

Blissed-out or bored, miraculous or banal, alive-with-interest or utterly numb, it's up to your perspective. Are you cultivating clarity in a daily way? What helps you *polish the mirror* of your mind? What helps you shed the dust of ignorance, greed and hatred?

Day 88

"It is one of the blessings of old friends that you can afford to be stupid with them." ~ *Ralph Waldo Emerson*

Which friend comes to mind when you think about being stupid together? Can you call that friend right now and play a truly idiotic prank on them or at least leave a silly song on their answering machine?

Day 89

"The artist, after all, is not a special kind of person; every person is a special kind of artist." ~ Michael Michalko

If you valued yourself as an artist, what kind of art would you create? [P.S. if you don't resonate with the word artist, replace it with the word *inventor*].

Day 90

"Creating happiness became part of my identity and set the course for my future. To this day, seeking every opportunity for happiness remains a part of my daily life, and defines my personality." ~ Carl S.

What would you say defines your identity? Which daily rituals do you see as shaping your destiny?

Final Thoughts

"Be the seasons. Welcome change. Be the moon. Shine through the darkness. Be the pebble. Let time shape and smooth you. Be the leaf. Fall gracefully when your time comes to let go. Trust the circle. To end is to begin."
~ *Naomura*

Well, you've made it. You've kept your commitment to practice, in a daily way, cultivating clarity. Writing can help. Sitting quietly can support this habit, too. I would love to hear from you regarding what you found the most evocative for your soul. Can you start right now, trusting the power of your clarity?

Blessings on your way,

Jennifer L. Manlowe
Creative Career Consultant
Life Design Unlimited
Bainbridge Island (2008)

P.S. Please write to me with your own favorite quotes, questions or comments through my webpage:
www.mylifedesignunlimited.com